SECRET Codes for Kids

BURTON ALBERT, Jr.

Illustrated by Dev Appleyard

Albert Whitman & Company, Chicago

To
ALMA DOW
whose love and goodness
are no secret.

Library of Congress Cataloging in Publication Data

Albert, Burton, Jr.
    Codes for kids.

    Includes index.
    SUMMARY: Explains and illustrates twenty-nine
codes which can be used to send secret messages or
as brainteasers.
    1.   Ciphers—Juvenile literature.   [1.   Ciphers]
I. Appleyard, Dev.   II. Title.
Z103.3.A53   001.54'36   76-25456
ISBN 0-8075-1239-7

Second Printing 1981

What's more fun than keeping a secret? Of course—it's finding one out! This book, **Codes for Kids,** helps you do both.

There are twenty-nine codes here. The key for each code is given to show you how to write in that code. Try the key. Crack the practice codes to make sure you understand the secret. Check the messages you decode with the Answer File which begins on page 30.

What can you do with codes? Send passwords, warnings, and secrets to special friends and club members. Tell a coded diary how you feel and tuck away memories you want to keep for you alone to read. Put a code on a bulletin board or chalkboard as a brainteaser—perhaps you can puzzle some adults while you're at It.

WARNING: Never write a code and its meaning on the same piece of paper. That's like handing the key to spies and inviting them to break every coded message you send. Treat this code book as a book of secrets and keep it free of marks and writing. Then nobody can trail you through **Codes for Kids.** Ready to go? Have fun!

Mirror, Mirror on the Wall

Mirror, mirror on the wall,
Who's the fairest one of all?

Will the mirror claim you're the fairest of all? Well . . . maybe. But it will surely crack the code here. The words are written backward—just hold them up to a mirror. See how the squiggles spell out some funny names of towns in different states? Is one the name of your hometown?

TRY THE KEY: CRACK THE CODES

1. BROKENARROWOKLAHOMA
2. BIRDSNESTVIRGINIA
3. HALFWAYOREGON
4. ZAPNORTHDAKOTA
5. GOOSEEGGWYOMING
6. BADAXEMICHIGAN
7. EEKALASKA
8. MONEYMISSISSIPPI
9. DOCTORTOWNGEORGIA
10. RIDDLEIDAHO
11. FRIENDNEBRASKA
12. WHATCHEERIOWA
13. WINKTEXAS
14. FINGERTENNESSEE
15. CLEVERMISSOURI
16. PAINTEDPOSTNEWYORK

How well did you do? See the Answer File on page 30.

This code is easy if you tuck the key into a corner of your brain: Each word in the secret message comes **AFTER** the name of an animal.

To keep snoopers off the track, you will need misleads. A *mislead* is a word or letter or mark which keeps the message hidden. Here's how it works.

Step 1   Write your message, leaving space between words.

Step 2   Write the name of an animal above each word in the secret message.

Step 3   Add misleads.

Step 1	Step 2	Step 3
		CAMEL
	CAMEL	MEETING
MEETING	MEETING	SINCE
		WELCOME
		AT
	KANGAROO	KANGAROO
CALLED	CALLED	CALLED
		HERE
		TO
		THE
	WHALE	WHALE
OFF	OFF	OFF
		LOST
		OUR
		WAY

TRY THE KEY: CRACK THE CODES

What message is hidden among the jungle of animals in each code?

1 BOB
  CALLED
  ELEPHANT
  BRING
  LUNCH
  SLEDS
  GIRAFFE
  CAMERA
  BREAKFAST
SNOW
BICYCLES
BUTTERFLY
TO
  HORSE
  MEETING
  SOON
  CAN'T
  COW
  ON
  I
    KITTEN
    MONDAY

2
DID
  BUFFALO
    LOUIS
      SEE
        CANARY
          IS
            TUESDAY
              OWL
                SICK
                  RAIN
                    LION
                      SEND
                        COOKIES
                          DUCK
                            CARD
                              BEACH
                                RABBIT
                                  TO
                                    VERY
                                      7:00
                                        GOOSE
                                          HOSPITAL
                                            TRAIN
                                              HENRY
                                                TODAY

3 ARE
  YOU
  MOUSE
  LET'S
    ROBIN
      GO

INTO NOW WILL FOX TO THESE MONKEYS
                                THE
                              SAILING
                              PUPPY
                              CIRCUS

WARNING: Write the secret words on a separate piece of paper. Keep coded messages in this book hidden from the kids who will trail you.

Inchwords

Place a ruler on a piece of paper. Draw a line at the left end of the ruler. Above the half-inch marks, print the letters in your message. Circle the last letter.

B E W A R E O F S P Y
1 2 3 4 5 6

Set traps for snoopers with misleads. Add letters to spell real or nonsense words which have nothing to do with the message.

IS BOB FREE? WHY ALL RUB - ELSE ONE FISHES UP TO YOU

If you have a metric ruler, use centimeters for coding.

K E E P O U R S E C R E T
METRIC 1 2 3 4 5 6 7 8 9 10 11 12 13 14 15

Set traps with misleads.

ASK ME EXPLORE USE RUSTED CORNER TONIGHT

TRY THE KEY: CRACK THE CODES

Get a ruler with inches, line it up with the mark at the left.

1 ROB 23 I LOOK ME I FELL OVER YES 36 AMY LOVE YOU

2 IS TOM ONE I SEE AT 3 AMY TOO CAN ALL VOTE NOW

Get a metric ruler, use centimeters for decoding.

3 WHICH DO ALL LIKE ACE TRICKS AND RED SPADES

4 TWO ARE IN THE FLOWER SAMMY AT TRAIN COOK

Save your ice cream sticks—they make super code-breakers, too. Notch one stick, then notch others in the same way. Hand them to friends who will share your secret key.

    Draw a line at the left end of the stick. Print a letter in each notch. To signal the last letter, slant or slash it.

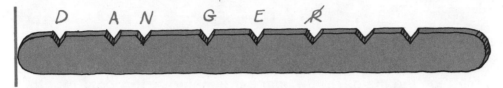

And to snuff out snoops, stuff spaces with misleads.

TRY THE KEY: CRACK THE CODES

Trace this outline of an ice cream stick. Cut it out and lick away the mystery that coats each message below.

The last letter in the message is *SLANTED* or *SLASHED*

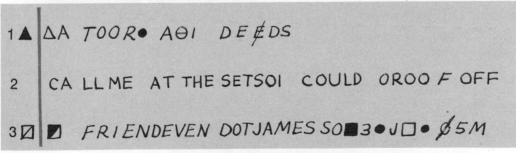

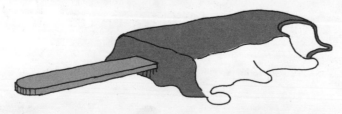

Ship messages inside a paper clip. Mark your starting point with a line, like this

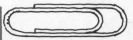

Slip the first letter of your message in the smaller opening of the clip, like this

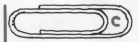

Now move the clip until the letter you've just written shows at the left, on the inside. In the smaller opening at the right, put the second letter of your message, like this

Then slip the clip again and write the third letter:

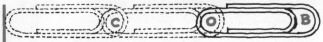

Repeat for each letter in your message. Finally, signal the last letter by writing a numeral after it.

C   O   B   R   A5

Fill in spaces with misleading shapes and letters.

■ Ø BEACH SAILORS IN BUGGY RACE TEA5 NOON

When you try this code, you might write each coded message on a long, narrow strip of paper. Rolled up, the paper can be easily passed to the receiver.

TRY THE KEY: CRACK THE CODES

1 | WHEN I CAN TRY ■ SCOUTS ■ OR ★ MUSIC ■ ME3

2 | OLD| RAILROAD CARS HIS MIKE ⊗ THERE RED6!

3 | FAST CAT ◦ ALONE FOR ONE ◦ CUTS 5 TREES

4 | TASTE OUR TREAT ■ IS ORDER AWAY 9©

Pictograms

You can use pictures to write messages. Each picture means what you want it to, a single word or a group of words.

Sketch a picture of each word or word-group you need to weave into a message.

a	✓	Cindy	Cd	have	◒	school	▱	to →
after	↶	club dues	∉	i	◉	snack	♉	tomorrow ✕
am	▲	clubhouse	⌂	is	∅	soon	◡	we ∞
and	+	for	4	Kiki	⟩K	tell	∿	with ++
are	Я	going	⊗∞⊗	meet at	→←	the	•	yes ◡
bring	↲	hamburger	⊖	no	⌒	there	⟨	you ☻

Then write pictograms. For example, Cd ∅ ⊗∞⊗ → • ⌂ means *Cindy is going to the clubhouse.*

TRY THE KEY: CRACK THE CODES

1 →← • ▱

2 ⟩K ∅ ++ Cd

3 ↲ ✓ ♉ → • ⌂ ✕

4 ⟩K + Cd Я ⊗∞⊗ ⟨ ◡

5 Я ∞ → ↲ ∉

6 ◡ →← • ⌂ ✕

7 ◉ ▲ ⊗∞⊗ → ◒ ✓ ⊖ ↶ ▱

8 ◉ ◒ • ∉ 4 ☻

Stack 'Em

Here's a code that's built like two stacks of ABC blocks.

First, write out your message and count the number of letters to find the midpoint.

Now stack the letters in two towers, like this,

To begin coding the message, start at the top. Write each pair of letters across from each other.

NR EA WI TL

Here's the last step. Bunch the letters into sets of four. If you need to, add misleads to fill out the last set.

NREA WITL

To break this code, work backward. Stack one pair of letters under the next and read the message down, starting with the column on the left. Of course the message can have more than two words. Cross out the misleads.

TRY THE KEY: CRACK THE CODES

1 GDOI TMAE

2 YCOR UAAZ RYEQ

3 MAYY DSAN DOSJ

4 WRAT TRCO HUOB ULTE FXOJ

No matter how far it rambles or wriggles, a cornered code cannot slip past the sharp eyes of a person holding the right key. And this is it: **Each letter inside a corner forms part of a message. All other letters and marks are misleads.**

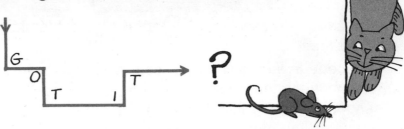

TRY THE KEY: CRACK THE CODES

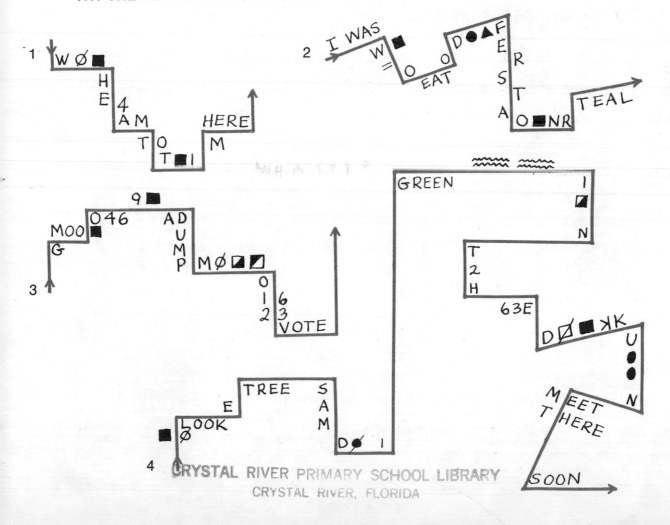

A mess! That's what you want spies to think if they unwind what looks like a wrinkled wad of paper.

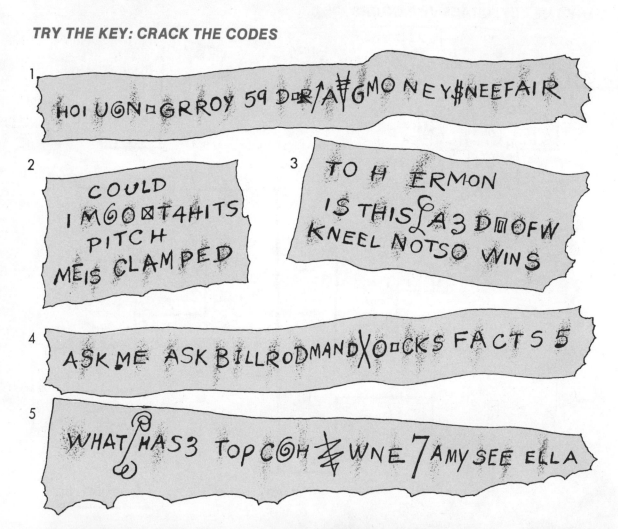

But look again at each smudgy letter. What tattletale trail do the smudges leave?

This code is easy if you print your message in pencil, leaving spaces between the letters. Rub a finger over each letter of your message, smudging it.   Play with misleads between smudges, then wrinkle the paper into a wad.

TRY THE KEY: CRACK THE CODES

In code families, cousins to Smudge & Wrinkle are the Easy Creases. Instead of being smudged, each letter or whole word in your message is written in the crease of a folded paper. Try a strip of paper, folded many times. When your message is finished, add misleads, being careful to avoid the creases.

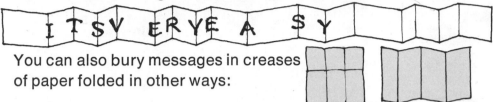

You can also bury messages in creases of paper folded in other ways:

Then by building a misleading message around the coded words, you nip any snoop in the snout!

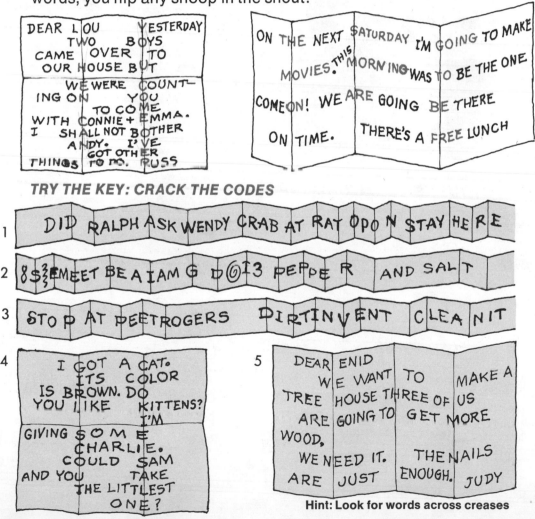

TRY THE KEY: CRACK THE CODES

Hint: Look for words across creases

Shopping Lists

At first glance, the words here seem to be a scribbled shopping list. There isn't a hint that the list could be anything else. Yet it is.

The **1** in the first line means count in *one* letter in *Dog Food.* Jot down the **D** on a paper. The **3** in the next line signals the **third** letter in *Hair Brushes,* which is **I**. The **1** before *Saw* clues you into jotting down the **S**.

What IS this? Remember, write the secret word on a separate piece of paper. Keep the coded messages in the book hidden!

1 Dog Food
3 Hair Brushes
1 Saw
2 Onions
4 Cakes
3 Keys
3 Milk
4 Sugar Pops!!
6 Raisin Bran
1 Dozen Donuts

TRY THE KEY: CRACK THE CODES

1

1 BLOUSE
2 LEMONS

3 SPOONS
1 NECKLACE

3 NUT-FLAKES
1 IVORY SOAP
1 MOP
4 BIKE BASKETS

2

5 Friskies
2 beans
3 Cheerios
1 Peanut Butter

4 marshmallows
6 coffee cups
4 dog chow
6 peppers
4 blueberries
4 tarts

3

1 tomato
2 cherries
2 cigars
5 cheese

1 salt
4 butter
2 figs
1 noodle bag
8 corn flakes
8 coconuts

4

1 NUTMEG
5 TURKEYS
4 POTATOES
1 ROOT BEER

1 EGG
8 JELLY ROLLS
1 MEATBALL

5 SUGAR
3 FLOUR
3 PLATES
3 TV DINNERS

A slightly different key is used in the next coded lists. The **first** number is the only one you will use. Pay no attention to other numbers. Look only at main words, not misleads like *1 doz., 2 pkg., 10¢, or 1 lb.*

For example, "2 eggs" means look at the second letter in **every** word in the list, beginning with *eggs.* Watch out for misleads! Only count letters in the main words—*eggs, donuts*—and so on.

2 eggs
1 doz. donuts
2 pkg. Glad Bags
address book
Afro Sheen
pie
4 ash trays
sheets

TRY THE KEY: CRACK THE CODES

1	2	3	4
3 cabbages	3 lemons	2 EYE DROPPERS	2 cat food
slippers	13¢ stamps	SOUP	starch
6 eggs	butter	BUTTER	5 chop suey
fudge	Schick blades	4 PLUMS	½ lb. cold cuts
seeds	lace	CORN	3 small onions
2 lb. clams	celery	ASPARAGUS	1 pkg. pecans
oil	1 lb. beans	1 LB. PEANUTS	
	baseball		
	cashews		

Swiss Cheese

You could use a thin slice of Swiss cheese for a grid to set up a secret message. But suppose a mouse nibbled your cheese? Better use a piece of paper, folded and cut this way:

Fold and snip

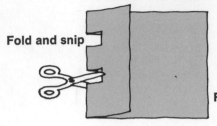

Fold and snip

Fold and snip

Open your riddled grid and lay it flat. Snip off the upper corner at the right.

Place the grid over a plain piece of paper, making sure the snipped corner is at the upper right. Write your message in the holes.

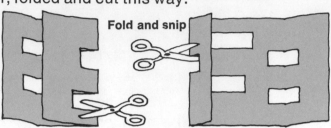

Lift the grid and put in misleads to tangle up the coded words.

Then by building a misleading message around the coded words, you nip any snoop in the snout!

I DID NOT DO MY MATH.
BUT YOU KNOW WHO DID!
LET ME TAKE OUT YOUR CAMERA
I WANT A PICTURE OF AN OLD BIKE
SHOWN AT THE MUSEUM TODAY

TRY THE KEY: CRACK THE CODES

On thin tracing paper, outline the grid shown here. Then place the grid over the messages and read the boxed words. See through the meaning!

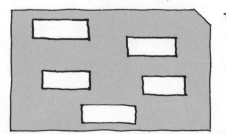

1

when will you be ready? I can stop with Tim to get you. I'll come as soon as the game is over.

2

Rick
Pete and I are going to hike with Hal. We lost our way the last time so look out for us.

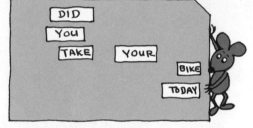

No, a computer didn't run wild and sputter out miles of gobbledygook. But that's what this code looks like to prying eyes.

Although it looks like a brain buster, it's as easy to figure out as flipping a top on soda pop.

Here's the key. **If a number begins a row, start with that number and count in that many places.** Note the letter. Do not count the dashes. If a letter starts a row, write down the letter. That's it!

2-C566-4N

HO-511

3-WI-6

CRT-0006-P

A-2

7-1-3-44-ZG

6003209

Try the sample code. The number **2** starts the first line. Count over two places, beginning with the **2** and skipping the dash. Your first letter is **C**. The next line has **no** number at the beginning, so you write down **H**. The following line starts with **3** and you count over three places to find the letter **I**. Now go on—blow away the rest of the misleads clouding the Windy City. What's its name?

TRY THE KEY: CRACK THE CODES

1	2	3	4	5
41CB-002	63-000RT	5N-32T	4-WWW-6	2N-663-0
7233-R2A	2UMN-619	206-55-N9	HN-2	E-1-2-66P
C444-001	NG-66-2230	MNT-0002	ADQ-6655	5004-XYD
2K1-6633			3-4T-NQ-900	TR-3
	5-11-60NP-T	3-NL-P-662		
411PQ-R	3-GF76-4W	350946	5000-A1	T-M-444
53-02APQ	FE-3-4N	V-62		4-BBU-9006
C25-2Y		3-CE-110-Q	BF-6F-FT	3-IE-87-IE
30K444-6		75444-CS-2	65991073	SMP-0-25
			R-2	7-000-59-D
TNX-3365		P 3	459-E-X-2208	ABC-4961
8436-99JR		400-IOU		2Y-I-9-66-LH
3BI-LN		ZT66-Y-23		
5006P-32		2Z-639		
		4-11A		

1-Up

To make the key for 1-Up, draw a line and string the letters of the alphabet above it. Then begin with **B** and write the alphabet below the line. End with **A**. Each code letter is "one up" from the message letter above it.

Message letters	A B C D E F G H I J K L M N O P Q R S T U V W X Y Z
Code letters	B C D E F G H I J K L M N O P Q R S T U V W X Y Z A

To use the key, think of each letter in your secret message, but write the letter below it. Letters for **PARADE** would march along like this, **QBSBEF**.

TRY THE KEY: CRACK THE CODES

1 **J DBO HP**
2 **GJMM CJSE GFFEFS**
3 **SJEF UIF QJOUP**

4 **HP GMZ B LJUF**
5 **MJHIUIPVTF JT FNQUZ**
6 **IPCCZ TIPQ TBMF**

7 **BTL FMJABCFUI**
8 **OP HZN UPEBZ**
9 **XIBU EP ZPV NFBO**

Scramble

In a code where one letter stands for another, you can mix up the letters in any way you want. These codes are different from 1-Up because only the holder of the key can uncode a message. See for yourself. Which Scramble breaks which message?

Message letters	A B C D E F G H I J K L M N O P Q R S T U V W X Y Z
Code letters	L D E A V M F B U C T O Q J K S W N Y X P I Z R H G

Message letters	A B C D E F G H I J K L M N O P Q R S T U V W X Y Z
Code letters	F R H Q X O P G N V W I J Z A S B T K C Y L D U M E

TRY THE KEY: CRACK THE CODES

1 **DUF MUFBX**
2 **CGFZWKPNLNZP**
3 **RFTRNX QAIIK**

4 **AKJX XNUS PS**
5 **EBUOU LJA XLEKY**
6 **HTM RFRM**

7 **FOPV XBV SOLJV**
8 **YWPVLOVN**
9 **UJ XBV BLOOZLH**

This code works like 1-Up, but has a different twist. It uses the **first** letter of the name of the person who will receive the message. If you are passing a secret to Liang, **L** is the important letter. Here's how it works.

Print your top alphabet in color, from **A** to **Z**. Take a strip of paper twice as long as this alphabet and print two complete alphabets, one after the other.

TROUBLE SPACING LETTERS EVENLY? TRY THIS!

DROP YOUR LETTERS BETWEEN DOTS

ABCDEFGHIJKLMNOPQRSTUVWXYZ

XYZABCDEFGHIJKLMNOPQRSTUVWXYZ

To encode a message for Liang, slide the strip under the alphabet printed in color. The **L** should be under **A**. Go on just as you did in 1-Up or Scramble.

ABCDEFGHIJKLMNOPQRSTUVWXYZ

JKLMNOPQRSTUVWXYZABCDEFGHIJKLMN

If you're sending a message to Ann or Antonio, don't line up **A** under **A** or you'll be sending plain English. Line up **Z** under **A** instead.

TRY THE KEY: CRACK THE CODES

Remember, pay attention to the name of the person who gets the message.

1 *Liang* **MFJ RFX**
2 *David* **DOO LV VDIH**
3 *Vera* **NVOPMYVT XJJFJPO**
4 *Howard* **SBTILYFHYK WVDDVD**
5 *Suki* **FG GFW SFKOWJWV**
6 *Abby* **RHW NBKNBJ**
7 *Felix* **XJQQ NY**
8 *Orlando* **AWBR MCIF PIGWBSGG**
9 *Ursula* **LOH BIGY**
10 *Chad* **PGCV**

Gibberish? Letter dropouts? Doodles? What IS this? These questions might pop into mind if you saw

•   V   E A   S   I   H   A   P E   P

Place a tape-teller above the letters and you can crack the code as easily as reading the ABCs.

•Z M W C L D E K I Y J O R A N Q S B T P F G U V H X

•   V   E A   S   I   H   A   P E   P

And that's exactly what you do. Look at the tape-teller—it begins with a dot to help you line it up with the message. The tape-teller has all the letters of the alphabet in mixed-up order. Find **A** on the tape-teller and jot down the letter below it in the code. Find **B** and jot down the letter under it. The third letter is under **C**, and so on. The secret message begins "Hav--." What's the rest?

TRY THE KEY: CRACK THE CODES

•X S B C F G K Q R Z J A L D E H P T M I O U W N V Y

```
1  •    O M U N        H   E R
2  •    H Y N T        W   C A I
3  •    E T A V I    P L C S H E    N A C    I
4  •    I D U R E    N R B E O D Y  U U G    G
5  •    R F Y T E O S O  Y I U O U L E R L L B Y  L
```

•4 •19 •3   *17 Septillion*   2 •8 •25

Numbers can stand for letters. In the simplest key, the numbers go from 1 to 26. Backward, **26** could stand for **A**, **1** for **Z**.

A	B	C	...	X	Y	Z
1	2	3		24	25	26

A	B	C	...	X	Y	Z
26	25	24		3	2	1

Those are just two possible keys. Imagine! You can arrange the 26 numbers in 17 septillion ways—that's 17,000,000,000,000,000,-000,000,000. So it's important that you and receivers have the key being used.

For the codes below, here's the key.

A	B	C	D	E	F	G	H	I	J	K	L	M	N	O	P	Q	R	S	T	U	V	W	X	Y	Z
9	20	8	3	17	2	18	21	16	1	15	22	24	14	4	13	5	19	6	25	12	11	7	26	23	10

The dots separate the numbers in each word. Two dots separate words from each other. Three dots end a sentence.

1 **6.8.9.19.23**

2 **3.19.9.18..19.9.8.17**

3 **20.17..24.23..2.19.16.17.14.3**

4 **24.16.15.16..21.9.6..13.17.25..13.17.22.16.8.9.14**

5 **3.17.9.19..3.16.9.19.23..**
   20.17.6.25..3.9.23..17.11.17.19...
   24.16.6.6..13.4.22.6.15.16..22.4.11.17.3..
   25.21.17..13.12.13.13.17.25..13.22.9.23..
   16..7.19.4.25.17...4.12.19..8.22.9.6.6..
   16.6..13.12.25.25.16.14.18..16.25..4.14...

Foxy Boxes

Print your message:

MAP HIDDEN UNDER FRONT STEP

Box in each set of 5 letters. If your last box has fewer than 5 letters, add misleads.

MAP HI DDEN UN DER FR ONT S TEP RW

Now be sly as a fox. Write each group of letters backward. Then **MAPHI** will be **IHPAM**. Do the same with the other boxes.

IHPAM UNEDD FREDN STNOR WRPET

1	IPART CTESS	6	CDNIF BCIMO ASKOO
2	TARIP NOWSE KEMAG	7	STAHT TAEHC RAGNI
3	PMATS SROFS OTELA FQYAD	8	HTNEK HSKNI OTSIE FDHGU
4	GNIRB EMMAH SDNAR PIEWA	9	ESROH RKCAB NEEDI
5	FEULB REGNI GLIAN OYSTE TONIU	10	EVAHI IAPOT EHTTN JDEHS

Go By the Book

Between the covers of a book lies the key to the Schoolmate Code. Using copies of the same book (it could be a schoolbook), the sender and receiver work with messages made up of triplets.

A **triplet** has three parts, made up of numerals, like this:

76 - 9 - 6

The first number in a triplet stands for a page in the book.

76th page

The second number signals the line to look for on the page.

9th line

The last number shows how many words you are to count in from the left.

6th word

•76   *Tree House Myst*

think someone boarded up part of the attic? why?"

"Let's find out," Jeffrey said.

"Make a hole," Sammy suggested.

Benny held up his hand. "Wait," he said. "Le all along here. You can run your hand over th and maybe you can feel something."

It was Sammy who said, "Something is
• here, Benny. There's a long crack. Wh mean?"

"Another crack over

TRY THE KEY: CRACK THE CODES
To read the messages, use pages in this book.

```
1   4-3-5   19-11-3   6-4-4   20-1-1.   10-1-4   17-1-6
2   25-8-6   4-5-1   6-1-2   12-3-9
3   12-1-7   17-12-1   28-2-5   20-8-13   18-1-3   13-8-3
4   19-3-13   22-3-7   4-5-1   18-2-2   4-1-1
5   25-8-6   4-5-1   26-2-4   28-2-6   17-7-3   19-2-8
6   15-2-11:   13-6-4   17-9-5   18-3-1   28-3-5   28-8-4
7   25-3-1   16-2-1   28-2-10   19-5-5   17-17-10
```

The Zigzagger gets its name from the first step you take in writing with this key.

Step 1   Zigzag letters of your message: **CORN BEEF SANDWICH**

Step 2   Count the letters to see if the number can be divided by 4. If not, add misleads until you have a number that can be divided by 4.

Step 3   Take the letters from the top row, writing them in sets of 4. Leave a wide space, then write the letters from the bottom row, also In sets of 4.

Top row:	*Bottom row:*
CRBE SNWC	**ONEF ADIH**

For quick, easy decoding use two crayons, markers, or pencils of different color. A drawing pencil that's red at one end and blue on the other would be perfect.

Write the first two sets of letters in one color, leaving space between the letters, like this:

    C   R   B   E   S   N   W   C

Now squeeze the second set of letters into the empty spaces, using another color, like this:

    C O R N B E E F S A N D W I C H

Can you read the message? Remember, some messages may have several misleads to fill out the last spaces. Pay no attention.

TRY THE KEY: CRACK THE CODES

1	BSEB LGMQ AKTA LAEX	6	SXOE IDZN
2	WASO HMWR HTFR OEOK	7	KECO EPOL
3	GMRC IEEE YPAT CHRZ	8	IAEO AYIE HVTB BSTB
4	SOBL FGTB NWAL IHTM	9	DNBT EWTI OTOH RIHT
5	TATH MRHA LWTE OSTE ASML OSBR	10	ISNH NETO TOCA NLWQ

Freckles

Freckles can make a quick-and-easy key. Thirteen numbers and signs with 'freckles' can turn out this quick-and-easy key.

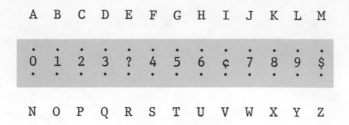

A B C D E F G H I J K L M

0 1 2 3 ? 4 5 6 ¢ 7 8 9 $

N O P Q R S T U V W X Y Z

FRECKLES CODE?

THEY MEAN A DALMATIAN CODE!

The freckle above signals one letter. The freckle below signals a different letter. For example, **8** with a freckle above it, like this **8̇** stands for **K**. If the **8** tiptoes on a freckle, like this **8̣** , the letter is **X**. Simple, isn't it?

TRY THE KEY: CRACK THE CODES

1   4̇ 5̣ 6̣ 2̣ ¢̇ 3   ¢ 3 ? 0̇

2   6̇ 1̣ 7   2̇ 6 ? 0̇ 2   2̇ 0 0   9 1̇ 6   5̇ ? 5̣

3   3̇ 1̣   9 1 6   7 0 0 5   5̣ 1 $̣ 0 8̇ ?   0̇   4̣ ¢ 9 $ 4̣ 5 ? ¢̇ 2

4   6̇ 1̣ 1̣ ? 0̇ 9   9 1 6 ¢̇ ?   2̇ ? 0̣ 2 8̇ ? 3   5 6̣ ?   2̣ 1 3 ?

5   2̣ ¢̇ 2 8   0̇   2̣ ? ¢̣ $?   4̇ ? 1 $ 5 6̣ ?   5̣ ? 0̇ 1   1̇ 0̇ 5

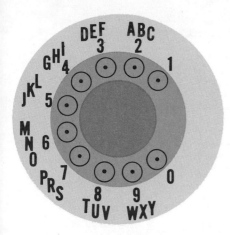

Tick-a-digit, tick-a-digit, tick-a-digit! Write a code by ticking the digits—the numbers—on a telephone dial or a Touch-Tone phone.

There are three letters for each number, except **1** and **0**. Here's how you use the letters and numbers to send a code. Write the number, then put a tick mark over it to show whether it is the first, middle, or last letter you mean.

6̀-M 6̇-N 6́-O

Because there is no **Q** or **Z**, use the number **1** to stand for **Q** and **O** to stand for **Z**.

TRY THE KEY: CRACK THE CODE

3̀ 3̇ 2 7   3̀ 4́ 2̀ 7́ 9́,   7́ 2̀ 4́ 6̀   2̀ 5 5   3̀ 2̀ 9.   6̀ 6   4̇ 2̀ 6̀ 3̀.

9̀ 3́ 6̀ 8̀   8̀ 6   7́ 4̇ 6̀ 9̀.   6̀ 6̀ 8̀   2́ 2̀ 3.

Telecode

How fast can you crack each coded message below? Aren't these just lists of telephone numbers? See for yourself. Take the last digit in each telephone number and count in from the left.

Count 8 Liz Metzger OR4-2968 /G
Count 2 Joe Svec 676-3762 /O

TRY THE KEY: CRACK THE CODES

1	2	3
Andy Bishop 227-4163	Tad Winslow HI2-6634	RED'S CAFE 833-6015
Lois Gray BI6-4458	Hairdresser HI2-5501	MARKET 833-9162
Dr. Nathan 227-5903	Aunt Alma 763-4725	CY MULLER GR5-0088
Tom Angelo 227-0004	Taxi HI2-9401	GLORIA GR5-6174
Maxie's Deli 226-9311	B. Lanetti 763-0066	AL'S GR5-0931
The Drive-In BI6-7209	Dentist 764-9775	POLICE 833-4533
Linda Betts 226-0968	Armando's Rest. HI6-9333	HOSPITAL 833-4998
Fire Dept. 226-5984	Emily 764-8381	MRS. BREYER GR5-2037

By sorting the alphabet into three tic-tac-toe frames you can shape the key to another puzzler. Here it is—

A	B	C
D	E	F
G	H	I

J̇	K̇	L̇
Ṁ	Ṅ	Ȯ
Ṗ	Q̇	Ṙ

S̤	T̈	Ṳ
V̤	Ẅ	X̤
Y̤	Z̈	?̈

In a coded message, each letter **A** through **I** is shown by the lines around the letter. For example, **A** is ⌋ , **E** is ☐ , **H** is ⊓ , and so on. Lines and dots stand for the rest of the alphabet letters, from **J**, ⌊• , to **Z**, •• .

TRY THE KEY: CRACK THE CODE

my secret diary   june 7

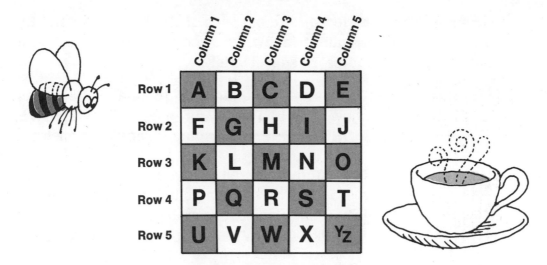

What's a 12 that stings? What's a 45 that's sipped?

With 25 little squares, you can quickly answer, "A bee (**B**) stings. And tea (**T**) is sipped." The squares make a checkerboard key.

To code a message, change each letter into a two-figure number. Then the letter **R** becomes **43**. The figure **4** is for *row 4*. The figure **3** means the *third column* over, moving from left to right. To decode **25**, find row 2 and run your finger over to column 5. You'll find **J**. Watch out for **55**—it stands for either **Y** or **Z**, depending upon the rest of the message.

Two hints about writing in this code: leave space between the two-figure numbers to make them easy to read. Leave plenty of space between words, and use punctuation if you wish.

TRY THE KEY: CRACK THE CODES

```
1   23 35 51 44 15   24 44   23 11 51 34 45 15 14
2   53 15   53 15 34 45   44 34 35 43 31 15 32 24 34 22   35 21 21
    45 23 15   24 44 32 11 34 14
3   53 23 35   22 11 52 15   55 35 51   45 23 15   13 23 11 43 33
    12 43 11 13 15 32 15 45
4   53 23 55   14 24 14   45 23 15 55   44 42 51 15 11 32 ?
```

Here's a good code for short messages of 16 or fewer letters. By agreeing upon the trail to follow, you and your friend can wind the way through a forest of secret letters.

Divide a large square into 16 small squares, as shown here. Print your message **WE HAVE MONDAY OFF** in the squares, adding a mislead.

Now study the trail you will use to code your message. The star marks the beginning, the dot is the end. Using this trail, your message will look like this: **WVNO EEDF HMAF AOYQ**

For easy decoding, draw a square with 16 small squares. Following the trail map, put the code into the boxes and read the message. Cross out the mislead.

TRY THE KEY: CRACK THE CODES

Ready to follow new trails and uncover secret meanings? Take paper and pencil and begin each code by drawing a box with 16 squares in it. Fill in the letters, following the trail map for that code. Write the message out, breaking the letters into words.

Put the first letter of the coded message where you see the star. It marks the beginning. The dot is at the end. Follow the arrows!

1 to 4	5	6	7	8

1	LGTO	EOHD	TTEE	SORO	5	RRES	OHDE	VETR	CSRI
2	BGEC	RILO	INEP	NTSE	6	PEHC	LOIE	NSUU	BSOC
3	WHLE	ARER	TORB	CLDY	7	LMOC	YSRR	STIE	ENTG
4	KNAB	AHNI	RAEK	ESWE	8	DNSA	ITLE	OOHT	NEAC

Jefferson's Nose

The third President of the United States can help you send—or sniff out—a coded message. Here's how to do it.

1 Draw a light pencil line straight across a piece of paper.

2 Find a nickel and look closely at the outline of Mr. Jefferson's head.

3 Put the nickel on the pencil line with the tip of Jefferson's hair at the back touching the line. Slide the nickel from left to right as you print your message a letter at a time under the tip of Jefferson's nose.

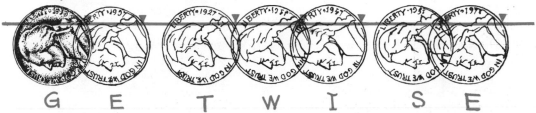

G   E   T   W   I   S   E

Put a tick mark on the pencil line at the tip of Jefferson's hair each time you move the coin. Sometimes move the nickel just a little, sometimes nudge it more.

4 Use as many lines as you need for your message. Use misleads to hide your meaning, and then erase all lines except the tick marks. The code can't be broken without them.

GO EAST TO WILLIE'S STEPS

TRY THE KEY: CRACK THE CODES

Dig up a nickel. Root out the meanings.

1 ▼   ▼   ▼   ▼   ▼   ▼   ▼

A I T Q M S V H I A W T J P S X S A L I M L T Z

2   ▼   ▼   ▼   ▼   ▼   ▼

M O N D A Y ● ⑤ T R A P O U T Ø M ▣ O R C R A C E R ▨

Answer File

Mirror, Mirror on the Wall, page 4
1 BROKEN ARROW, OKLAHOMA
2 BIRDSNEST, VIRGINIA
3 HALFWAY, OREGON
4 ZAP, NORTH DAKOTA
5 GOOSE EGG, WYOMING
6 BAD AXE, MICHIGAN
7 EEK, ALASKA
8 MONEY, MISSISSIPPI
9 DOCTORTOWN, GEORGIA
10 RIDDLE, IDAHO
11 FRIEND, NEBRASKA
12 WHAT CHEER, IOWA
13 WINK, TEXAS
14 FINGER, TENNESSEE
15 CLEVER, MISSOURI
16 PAINTED POST, NEW YORK

Jungle Jumble, page 5
1 BRING CAMERA TO MEETING ON MONDAY.
2 LOUIS IS SICK. SEND CARD TO HOSPITAL.
3 LET'S GO TO THE CIRCUS.

Inchwords, page 6
1 BIKE FOR SALE
2 MEET AT CAVE
3 COLLECT CARDS
4 WAIT FOR MY TRICK

Popsticklers, page 7
1 TRADE
2 LET'S SURF
3 FEED JOJO

Clip-Slip, page 8
1 IT'S TRUE
2 ASK TED
3 CANOES
4 TUESDAY

Pictograms, page 9
1 Meet at the school.
2 Kiki is with Cindy.
3 Bring a snack to the clubhouse tomorrow.
4 Kiki and Cindy are going there soon.
5 Are we to bring club dues?
6 Yes. Meet at the clubhouse tomorrow.
7 I am going to have a hamburger after school.
8 I have the club dues for you.

Stack 'Em, page 10
1 GOT A DIME
2 YOU ARE CRAZY
3 MY DAD SAYS NO
4 WATCH OUT FOR TROUBLE

Corner It! page 11
1 WHAT TIME?
2 WOOD FORT
3 GOOD MOVE
4 LET'S DIG IN THE DUNES

Smudge & Wrinkle, page 12
Example: YOU FOUND IT
1 HUNGRY DRAGON NEAR
2 MOTH ESCAPED
3 THE SHADOW KNOWS
4 SEABIRD DOCKS AT 5
5 WATCH WEASEL

Easy Creases, page 13
Examples: WHEN CAN YOU COME OVER?
THE MOVIES ON SATURDAY
MORNING ARE GOING TO BE FREE.
1 VIPER STRUCK
2 DRAW CARTOONS
3 SEE BIG DIPPER
4 PAPER DRIVE
5 GIRL SCOUT COOKIE SALE
6 WE NEED THREE MORE NAILS

Shopping Lists, page 14
Example: DISNEYLAND
1 BE ON TIME
2 KEEP SECRET
3 THIS STINKS
4 NEAR ELM ROAD

More Shopping Lists, page 15
Example: GOLDFISH
 1 BIG DEAL
 2 MATH CLASS
 3 YOU LOSE
 4 AT HOME

Swiss Cheese, page 16
 1 WHEN CAN YOU COME OVER?
 2 PETE AND HAL LOST OUT

Brainbuster, page 17
Example: CHICAGO
 1 BACKPACK TRIP
 2 RUN OFF
 3 TOM LOVES PIZZA
 4 WHAT A BORE
 5 NEXT TUESDAY

1-Up, page 18
 1 I CAN GO
 2 FILL BIRD FEEDER
 3 RIDE THE PINTO
 4 GO FLY A KITE
 5 LIGHTHOUSE IS EMPTY
 6 HOBBY SHOP SALE
 7 ASK ELIZABETH
 8 NO GYM TODAY
 9 WHAT DO YOU MEAN?

Scramble, page 18
First Scramble breaks 1, 4, 5,
7, 8, 9; second 2, 3, 6
 1 BIG FIGHT
 2 THANKSGIVING
 3 BARBIE DOLLS
 4 DON'T TRIP UP
 5 CHILI AND TACOS
 6 CRYBABY
 7 GLUE THE PLANE
 8 SQUEALER
 9 IN THE HALLWAY

Now You're Up! page 19
 1 BUY GUM
 2 ALL IS SAFE
 3 SATURDAY COOKOUT
 4 LUMBERYARD POWWOW
 5 NO ONE ANSWERED
 6 SIX O'CLOCK

 7 SELL IT
 8 MIND YOUR BUSINESS
 9 RUN HOME
10 NEAT

Tellertape, page 20
Example: HAVE A PEPSI
 1 HOME RUN
 2 WHY CAN'T I?
 3 LET'S HAVE A PICNIC
 4 RIDE OUR DUNE BUGGY
 5 IF YOU TELL YOU'LL BE SORRY

17 Septillion, page 20
 1 SCARY
 2 DRAG RACE
 3 BE MY FRIEND
 4 MIKI HAS PET PELICAN
 5 DEAR DIARY
    BEST DAY EVER.
    MISS POLSKI LOVED
    THE PUPPET PLAY
    I WROTE. OUR CLASS
    IS PUTTING IT ON.

Foxy Boxes, page 21
 1 TRAP IS SET
 2 PIRATES WON GAME
 3 STAMPS FOR SALE TODAY
 4 BRING HAMMER AND SAW
 5 BLUE FINGERNAIL GETS
    YOU IN
 6 FIND COMIC BOOKS
 7 THAT'S CHEATING
 8 KEN THINKS HE IS TOUGH
 9 HORSEBACK RIDE
10 I HAVE TO PAINT THE SHED

Go by the Book, page 22
 1 You're sending snoopers gibberish.
    That's wild.
 2 You are a tattletale.
 3 Spies try to find the building.
 4 Important messages are above
    the mirror.
 5 You are to follow the key person.
 6 Attention: bury letter below
    forest trail.
 7 Telephone secret friend in city.

TOP SECURITY

Zigzagger, page 23

1 BASKETBALL GAME
2 WHAT'S FOR HOMEWORK?
3 GYM PRACTICE HERE
4 SNOWBALL FIGHT
5 TOAST THE MARSHMALLOWS
6 SIX DOZEN
7 KEEP COOL
8 I HAVE TO BABYSIT
9 DON'T BOTHER WITH IT
10 IT'S ON CHANNEL TWO

Freckles, page 24

1 STUPID IDEA
2 HOW CHEAP CAN YOU GET?
3 DO YOU WANT TO MAKE A FILMSTRIP?
4 HOORAY, YOU'VE CRACKED THE CODE
5 PICK A PRIZE FROM THE GRAB BAG

Dial-a-Code, page 25

DEAR DIARY,
RAIN ALL DAY
NO GAME. WENT TO SHOW.
NOT BAD.

Telecode, page 25

1 DYNAMITE
2 WHAT TIME?
3 CAR RALLY

Tic-Tac-Code, page 26

DEAR DIARY,
TODAY I TURNED TEN.
HAD SURPRISE PARTY.
WE PLAYED GAMES AND
ATE AT MC DONALD'S.
THE DAY WAS WARM
AND SPECIAL.
TREASURE IT FOREVER,
MY SECRET FRIEND.

Checkerboard, page 27

1 HOUSE IS HAUNTED
2 WE WENT SNORKELING OFF THE ISLAND
3 WHO GAVE YOU THE CHARM BRACELET?
4 WHY DID THEY SQUEAL?

Letter Trails, page 28

1 LET'S GO TO THE RODEO
2 BRING IN TELESCOPE
3 WATCH ROLLER DERBY
4 KAREN HAS A NEW BIKE
5 CROSS THE RED RIVER
6 CLUBHOUSE IS OPEN
7 LOST MY SECRET RING
8 CANOE TO THE ISLAND

Jefferson's Nose, page 29

1 THAT'S IT
2 NO MORE

Index